# Making Academic Presentations

What Every University Student Needs to Know

Robyn Brinks Lockwood
Stanford University

University of Michigan Press
Ann Arbor

■ Acknowledgments

Over the years, countless students have told me that standing in front of an audience to give a presentation makes them very nervous. I must admit that I often still feel some apprehension whenever I have to present in front of an audience, and my students are doing this in their second language. I commend them for taking my classes, often of their own volition, to make themselves better speakers and presenters. I look forward to hearing all their success stories. I am grateful for their attendance, participation, and initiative in my classes. I also want to acknowledge Kelly Sippell, my first editor at University of Michigan Press, who listened to my own presentation about why I wanted to write this book and supported me through the first stages of the writing process. Thanks also to the editorial and production teams at University of Michigan Press for seeing this book to fruition. I must thank some members of my own personal audience. Thanks to my parents, Virgil and June; my husband, John; and my brother, Tim, for always being there no matter what ideas I was presenting. And, as always, I dedicate this to Darrin and Nathan, my nephews. I will always be front and center in their audiences.

Contents

■ Introduction

I teach English for Academic Purposes (EAP) courses for international students at the university level. One goal, of course, focuses on the E in EAP—my job is to teach English. But at the university level, many students already know English. They've achieved a level of fluency beyond what many of us ever achieve in our second languages. But another goal focuses on the A and P in EAP. I want my students to do well in my English class, but my job extends beyond helping them succeed in only my course. I need to prepare my students to succeed beyond the ESL classroom. They need to do well in their other academic classes as well. Their goal isn't necessarily to just learn English—it is to attend and graduate from an English-speaking university with an undergraduate or graduate degree in a field specific to their future career. And to do that, they need to be able to give presentations in their general requirement classes, major classes, and graduate programs.

I have taught a variety of courses with many different names: Oral Presentation, Effective Communication, Speech, Oral or Speech Communication. The list goes on. I also taught a variety of different types of speeches: informative, persuasive, demonstration or process, impromptu, introduction, data presentation, poster, and conference presentation, to name just a few. The speeches I assigned depended not only on the level and needs of my students, but also on how much time I had in class. I wanted the bulk of my class time to be reserved for presentations, not bogged down in the textbook content. As a result, I could never find that "perfect" book. I needed a book that would offer students the basic content they needed and that they could then apply to any variety of speeches. I didn't need or want a long, thick textbook filled with assignments that either did not suit my students' needs or that I simply did not have time for in class. I needed a brief textbook that focused on just what students would need to be able to deliver a good presentation.

In addition to students being able to give a good speech in my English class, I needed them to recognize that making presentations extends far beyond the ESL classroom. Many of my students were finding they would have to make presentations in their general education courses, such as an informative speech in a Speech 101 class, a presentation on the Incan Empire in history class, a demonstration of an experiment in science class, or a summary of a book or play in a literature course. My graduate students were having to make poster presentations, describe data and results from their lab work, give conference presentations, and introduce speakers at the university. Former students who visited me after graduation told me that they often gave presentations to managers or staff after completing their internships and often presented or proposed ideas during meetings long after they graduated. Students will need to be proficient at making presentations, and if I could teach them the skills they needed, they would be far more successful.

In the spring of 2020, students around the world were taking all their classes online, which changed the way we teach. What I learned, however, was that this did not necessarily change our course objectives. Presentations did not disappear, they just transitioned and were given online. I "attended" three conferences during the summer of 2020 for which I was a speaker. This meant I was simply a presenter on Zoom, Skype, or some other platform. Presentations were still key to sending my students on a successful path.

Also in the spring of 2020, I attended a former student's dissertation defense. Though I had attended many defenses in the past, this was the first one I watched on Zoom. Rather than making eye contact with everyone in the room, the presenter needed to make eye contact with the webcam. Rather than projecting his slides and being situated at the front of the room, he needed to share his screen. But the same concepts were still at play—eye contact, visual aids, and the moves or parts of a presentation were still necessary. I am proud to report that my student's defense went well. He passed after the closed session and graduated with his PhD. Through watching his experience, I realized that students still need to present, and this skill is vital to their success in a variety of settings. Whether we teach live in a classroom or online, we still need to teach content about how to make presentations. Class assignments and projects, confer-ences, interviews, meetings, and other types of presenta-tions will continue regardless of how much of our lives shift to virtual settings. The skills and language of pre-sentations will not disappear.

I found myself with my first free summer in many years since the COVID-19 pandemic forced the closure of my summer program. This unexpected time off gave me the time to think about online instruction and teach-ing presentation skills. I revisited some of the materials used in the summer program I manage, as well as the materials I use in the courses I teach during the aca-demic year. I identified similarities that all presentations include regardless of type, such as introductions, bodies, and conclusions, and realized I needed this general core knowledge in a book.

From there, I started talking with colleagues here at Stanford University in my own as well as other depart-ments. What types of presentations did they assign students? What were the requirements for those pre-sentations? What did they find their students needed to develop in order to give a good presentation in their class? What did students already do well? I expanded my own little research project by talking to second-language teachers in other programs as well as professors of other disciplines at other universities. The one thing I found to be true for everyone was this: None of us always used the same types of speech or presentation assignments. And most of us agreed that we wished we had more class time for students to give presentations rather than focusing on textbook content. The fact that we were so different in the types of presentations we assigned is what made us all the same.

How could I develop a textbook that everyone can use if we're all assigning different types of presentations? How could I even develop a book for myself when I might offer different types of speeches each term? I thought then about two other books I had written for University of Michigan Press: *Office Hours: What Every University Student Needs to Know* (2019) and *Leading Academic Discussions: What Every University Student Needs to Know* (2020). These titles were shorter than your average textbook, at approximately 120 pages, and less expensive, at about $20. They each looked at a speech event, office hours and academic discussions, and broke it into "moves" or parts. I included specific language for each move as well as information about pronunciation and non-verbal communication. In looking at my materials, I saw that academic presentations could be fashioned in the same way—I could break down the general skills and language needed for the moves of a presentation. The book on discussions was short enough that it would allow teachers to spend most of the class time, if desired, on actual discussion rather than talking about talking. Additionally, the book didn't try to choose what types of projects or discussions the students would participate in. There is a section of ideas for discussions and plenty of tasks, but this format allows instructors the freedom to choose what works best for their students that term or to use any of their own ideas alongside the content in the book. My students were always telling me how they hated buying expensive books, most of which they didn't use. These textbooks solve that problem.

That brought me back to my pandemic summer with no students and no program. I had the summer to get ready for the following academic year, which meant preparing for speaking courses. If I needed to plan presentation assignments and if I wanted to revise based on the moves of a presentation, it seemed worth the time to add a third book for students to use: *Making Academic Presentations: What Every University Student Needs to Know.*

In summary, this book evolved from years' worth of my own classroom content, information collected during office hours and course evaluations from students, discussions with colleagues at Stanford and other programs, videos of presentations ranging from students in second-language and other courses to professionals in the workforce, recordings of student presentations from my classes, stories from former students about their experiences in academic and professional settings after they left my classroom, and observations of presentations in a variety of departments across campus. I also included information about what my students were experiencing with presentations in their classes once they were all online, what my graduate students were experiencing with research group presentations and conferences, and what I was experiencing at my own conferences now set in virtual platforms.

After reviewing my notes, I outlined five moves that students need to recognize and use to deliver good presentations, as well as some language they need to navigate through the presentation and Q & A, whether in person or online. There is a wealth of tasks throughout the book to help students practice different features. The book also includes Presentation Analysis boxes that allow students to evaluate other presentations. Students are encouraged to choose a presentation to watch online, but these boxes can also be used for presentations on campus (online or in person). There are Start Personalizing boxes throughout the book so that students, if they are ready to, can start planning one of their own presentations. Sample projects are included in Part 4 that can be used or adapted, as can the rubrics and evaluation forms in the Appendix.

I hope students and instructors will find this book useful in their presentation classes, but I also hope students recognize that this language and skill set are transferable. Students will be able to use these skills in many classes, regardless of what major or discipline they choose to pursue after their ESL or presentation class, and even beyond that, when they present themselves in job interviews and eventually begin working in academia or industry. The need to present never goes away, so it's best to prepare our students well.

1

What Is a Presentation?

Defining a presentation is challenging. At its most basic, a presentation is sharing a topic with or giving information to an audience. Presentations can take many forms, serve many purposes, and happen in many settings. Some ideas are provided here, but this list is far from complete.

Examples of Types of Presentations

- Speeches or talks
- Demonstrations
- Panels
- Thesis or dissertation defenses
- Lectures
- Keynotes or plenaries

Examples of Purposes

- To inform
- To persuade

- To educate
- To motivate
- To entertain

Examples of Settings

- Classrooms
- Conferences
- Offices or workplaces
- Meetings

Speech events you might not have considered presentations actually are. For example, job interviews, sales pitches, debates, infomercials, and introducing speakers are types of presentations. Even answering questions in class or sharing your opinion during an academic discussion is a presentation of sorts. Social or less formal events are presentations as well, such as a date where you try to portray yourself in the best light. There are even some presentations that might rely more on non-verbal communication. Think about a science fair project you completed in elementary or high school, or poster presentations on campus or at conferences (though poster presentations often include verbal communication as well). Even this textbook is a non-verbal presentation. When you think about the definition—sharing information with an audience—presenting is something everyone does nearly every day.

Presenting online is just as important, especially since virtual communication became so prevalent during the COVID-19 pandemic. Not only did classes move online, but large-scale events like conferences also pivoted to online formats. These virtual platforms are also becoming more prevalent for job interviews, meetings, and social engagements. There are some good reasons to practice presenting online even if you also have in-person classes or meetings with your fellow students, professors, or supervisors. Why? Online communication has made our world smaller. We don't need to get on a plane to talk to someone in another country anymore. Rather, we can be on Skype, Zoom, Google Hangouts, FaceTime, or some other online medium. Sometimes being online might actually feel less intimidating if you are worried about speaking up in person. Participants may be more comfortable raising a virtual hand than they would be in person. Many online platforms have a chat box, and course management systems have a discussion strand, so some Q & A sessions might be managed partially in written format. Another advantage to these online presentations is those written responses might be more thoughtful since participants have time to consider and formulate their questions or responses.

Many online presentations still occur synchronously, so Q & A sessions will be live just as they were in class or would be at an in-person event. Other online presentations that are asynchronous, in which audience members watch at their leisure, need to be carefully constructed since audience members won't be able to ask questions later. Learning the moves and language commonly used in presentations along with a lot of practice will help you present well regardless of the presentation type, purpose, or setting.

Audience

Your audience is one of the first things you should consider before preparing for a presentation. Who will be listening? Of course your instructor is part of your audience, especially if you are in a presentation or speech class. But try to think beyond that. Here are some considerations:

1. Do the audience members know as much as you about the topic?
2. How much background do the listeners have or need?
3. What kind of vocabulary will the audience members know? Can you use technical vocabulary?
4. Where will this presentation take place?

Consider a civil engineering student studying the best materials to use to build bridges. This student is taking an oral presentation class as a general education requirement, and the first assignment is to tell his instructor and classmates about his field of study. These four considerations make a big difference. First, the other students are not all engineering students and certainly not all studying the same specific aspect of civil engineering. Therefore, they likely need some background on bridges and materials. They also won't be as familiar with the technical words, so he will have to adjust his vocabulary. He needs to bear in mind that they are not an uneducated audience, though, which is common when making academic presentations, so he shouldn't "dumb down" his content. He shouldn't need to use sentences that are too simple, and some sentence complexity will not put the content out of reach. The speech will happen in class, meaning everyone there will be part of the academic community, so he shouldn't be too informal or too simplistic.

Now consider the same civil engineering student with the same topic, but now the presentation will be given at a professional conference for civil engineers. How do these considerations change what he might plan? First, the audience will be comprised of civil engineers. They might not have the same specific field of study, but they likely will attend his talk because they are interested in this specific topic. He should assume they have some background on bridges and materials, so less background will be required here. Because they are professional engineers, he can use more technical vocabulary throughout the presentation. These audience members are experts in the field. Since this is happening at a conference, it will be more formal.

TASK 1

Listen to this TED Talk and then answer the questions that follow. https://www.ted.com/talks/chris_anderson_ted_s_secret_to_great_public_speaking/transcript?referrer=playlist-before public speaking&language=en

1. Who do you think is Chris Anderson's intended audience? _____

2. Do you think his presentation reaches that intended audience? Why or why not?

   _____

3. Did you like this presentation? Why or why not? Do you think you are part of his intended audience? Does that influence whether someone enjoys a presentation?

   _____

   _____

   _____

Presentation Analysis

Find a presentation to analyze online. Don't worry about finding a perfect example. You will be using this sample for analysis, so it's okay if it is not good. It is helpful to pick one you are interested in, though, because you will be able to use this sample again throughout this textbook.

Be prepare to share the link with others in class and discuss these questions.

Who was the audience? _____

Did the presenter reach the intended audience? _____

Was there too much or too little background? _____

Was there too much or too little technical or unknown vocabulary? _____

Where did this presentation take place? _____

What could the presenter change to present the same topic to a different audience? For example, if the talk was intended for experts, how can it be changed to appeal to laypersons? _____

_____

Start Personalizing

What kinds of presentations do you give or anticipate you will have to give this year?

_____

_____

For each, who is the intended audience?

_____

_____

Choose a presentation you have given, will give, or want to give. Write a brief answer to each of the questions.

What is the title of the presentation? _____

What kind of presentation is it? _____

Do the audience members know as much as you about the topic? _____

How much background do the listeners have or need?

_____

What kind of vocabulary will the audience members know? Can you use technical vocabulary?

_____

Where will this presentation take place? _____

Purpose

When you are considering your audience, you also need to think about your purpose. Why are you giving this presentation? While you may want to simply answer "Because it is required" or "Because it is for a grade," try to think more deeply. What do you want the outcome of your presentation to be? Even if you want to earn an A grade, the best way to accomplish that is to make sure your presentation accomplishes its purpose. Do you want to inform, persuade, educate, motivate, or entertain?

Think about a commercial or infomercial you have seen online or on television. The purpose of this type of presentation is to sell the audience members the product or service—to persuade them. The purpose of a lecture you listen to in another class is to give you information that you need to understand the field—to inform you.

Some presentations might have more than one purpose. For example, the purpose of a process or demonstration could be to inform you, but it is also to teach you how to do something. The best presentations accomplish their purpose.

TASK 2

Think about Chris Anderson's TED Talk again.

1. What was Chris Anderson's purpose?

_____

2. Do you think he accomplished his purpose? Why or why not?

_____

_____

_____

3. Did he accomplish his purpose with you? Why or why not?

_____

_____

_____

_____

Presentation Analysis

Using the presentation of your choice, discuss these questions.

What was its purpose? _____

Where did this presentation take place? _____

Think of another purpose for the same speech. How would it change to serve a different purpose? For example, if the talk's intention was to inform someone about the presenter's opinion and persuade them to agree, it might need more statistics or examples to accomplish this.

_____

_____

_____

_____

_____

_____

_____

Start Personalizing

Think again about the presentations you listed in the
Start Personalizing box on page 14.

For each, what purpose do you hope to accomplish?

_____

_____

_____

Choose a presentation you have given, will give, or want
to give. Write a brief answer to each of the questions.

What is the title of the presentation? _____

What kind of presentation is it? _____

What is your purpose? _____

2

Presentation Moves

Presentations generally include three main parts: the opening or introduction, the body, and the conclusion. Your content will usually fall into those three categories; some will be at the beginning, most will be in the middle, and some will be at the end. Those sections also always occur in that order. Introductions are first, bodies are second, and conclusions are last. Listeners are expecting that general structure, and presenters should not stray from it. However, we want to study presentations in a little more depth, so we will study these three sections, but we will also incorporate visual aids and Q & A. For the most part, the content flows from beginning to end organized in such a way to appeal to your audience and accomplish your purpose. However, using visual aids in presentations is popular, and we will use them throughout all the sections. Therefore, although using visual aids is Move 3, you will notice the arrows pointing in both directions to indicate the fluidity of this move. You will also notice that

Move 5, the Q & A, comes after the conclusion. While Q & A generally falls at the end, think about a lecture you have heard. You've probably had teachers who stopped throughout the lecture and asked if there were questions. This move is also somewhat fluid. In more formal settings, such as a conference, the Q & A is almost always at the end of the presentation. It is important to (1) be familiar with the sections and moves, and (2) to know the language—verbal and non-verbal—you should use as you progress from part to part. The five moves are:

1. Starting the Presentation (the Introduction)
   ↓
2. Flowing through the Presentation (the Body)
   ↕
3. Using Visual Aids
   ↕
4. Concluding the Presentation (the Conclusion)
   ↓
5. Managing the Q & A

Throughout the moves and sections of presentations, we will cover suggested sentence frames and common language. While phrasing within each category or section tends to share the same general meaning or purpose, they may differ in directness, formality, and strength. Academic presentations are often "in the middle" in terms of formality. They tend to be less formal than writing but more formal than a conversation or social interaction. When you study each move and the corresponding language, think about which phrases are more or less formal and what is most appropriate for the audience, purpose, and setting of your presentation.

Move 1: Starting the Presentation (the Introduction)

Getting Attention

Move 1 is the usually first thing to happen to "officially" start the presentation, which is why it is listed at the top and has only a downward arrow extending from it. However, be aware that people might be talking before the presentation, especially if you are presenting at a conference or workplace. As people enter the room, there are greetings and perhaps even some small talk. If there is coffee or refreshments, people may be enjoying these offerings while discussing their weekends, the weather, or other events (classes, workshops, sessions). You can review some social interaction language to help you navigate this pre–Move 1 mingling, such as greetings, introductions, compliments, and small talk, especially if you are an audience member. Because of this socializing, the presenter might have to get people's attention before the official Move 1. For example, a presenter might say:

- I'm going to go ahead and start.
- Is everyone ready?

- Would everyone like to get some coffee and
  have a seat?
- Let's get started.
- Everyone, to stay on time, I'm going to begin.

Beginning Your Presentation

There are several ways you can begin your presentation, varying from traditional to very creative. You will
need to choose based on your audience and purpose. If
you are giving a presentation outside of class, you may
introduce yourself. You would not do this if you are in
a small class where everyone knows you. Some more
traditional examples might be similar to these:

- Today I'm going to introduce you to the
  shogun that played a large role in Japan's
  history between 1185 and 1868.
- Good morning. My name is Juan Melendez,
  and I am a graduate student studying
  electrical engineering at [university]. My
  presentation today will share data from my
  work on field programmable gate arrays
  being used in financial technology.
- I'd like to explain the best ways to invest
  your money.
- Hi everyone. I'm excited to be here today to
  demonstrate how easy it is to back up your
  computer safely and securely.

▦ Thank you for having me. My talk today is about emotional intelligence and why I think it is more important than IQ.

Indicating the Organization

After you let the audience members know the general topic, it is common to indicate how the body of the speech will be organized.

▦ Combine the organization with the opening statement.
  - My talk today will discuss the six levels of Bloom's taxonomy and give examples of learning objectives teachers might have for each level.
▦ Follow the opening statement with the organization.
  - Today I'm going to introduce you to the shogun that played a large role in Japan's history between 1185 and 1868. First, I'll explain what a shogun is and then talk about . . .
▦ Present the agenda or outline (verbally and/ or on a slide).
  - In my presentation, I will discuss my study, share the method I chose and why I chose it, talk about the population that participated in my study, show my results, and provide some interpretations and analysis of those details. I'll close with my ideas for future research.

Hooking the Listener

A hook is a device used to catch someone's attention. Depending on your audience and purpose, a hook is a good way to begin your presentation. There are several ways you can hook your audience members. Some ideas for hooks are listed here.

- Pose a question
  - Have you ever wished you could save more money without working? My presentation on solar power will show you how the average American can save hundreds of dollars a year.
    - Note: Most of these questions are rhetorical, meaning that the speaker does not require an answer and the audience members are not expected to answer. We use rhetorical questions to get the audience's attention, focus them on the topic, and make the topic relatable to the listeners.
- Pose a hypothetical
  - Imagine a world with no air pollution. What if I told you that I developed a process to reduce air pollution by nearly 70 percent?
- Make a claim
  - Fintech is the future of Wall Street and other financial markets around the globe.
- Tell a story or anecdote
  - When I was young, I wanted to . . .
  - My research in this area started by accident . . .

■ Use a visual aid or audio aid
  - Look at this picture. Does anyone know what this is?
  - Watch this video where the leading expert on flipped learning tells us what he believes will be the future of education.
  - I'm holding a [object].
  - Does anyone know what this is? [hold up object]
  - Listen to these sounds that whales make.
  - Watch this short video clip on flipped classrooms.

■ Use a quotation
  - The author of the book we studied says, "[Quote]." This quote alludes to the overall theme in the novel, and that will be the focus of my presentation.

■ Give statistics
  - Over 500 million people are estimated to have fallen victim to the Spanish flu in 1918. There were 50 million deaths, and almost 700,000 were in the United States. My presentation will focus on how pandemics can alter a country's population.

■ Provide background information
  - Definitions: Consumerism is the concept that encourages people to buy products and services in greater quantities.

- People: The Kennedy family has a long and storied history in American politics, service, and business.
- Process: Writing code is the process of creating instructions that can tell a computer what to do and how to do it.

Clarifying Your Purpose

Some presenters are forthright in stating or clarifying their purpose during Move 1. For example:

- By the end of my presentation, you'll see why solar power is well worth the initial output of money and time.
- After my demonstration, I think you will see how easy it is to install your own solar panels.
- When I finish, you will understand the role solar power plays in the city's overall environmental goals.
- I hope the information I share will motivate you to install solar panels on your own home.

TASK 3

Imagine you need to give a presentation on the environment. You can narrow the topic any way you like. Write three possible opening statements. You may choose three different strategies or use more than three in any combination.

- ▪ Traditional
- ▪ Indicating the Organization
- ▪ Hooking the Listener
- ▪ Clarifying Your Purpose

Examples:

- ▪ In my talk, I'm going to tell you about rainforests. I'll share the characteristics of a rainforest, talk about the animals and plants that live there, and show you some places where the rainforests are thriving.
- ▪ Did you know that some rainforests have existed for over 70 million years? Unfortunately, more and more are being destroyed. I hope that by the end of my talk, you'll agree that the rainforests are worth saving.
- ▪ Good morning. I want to begin by quoting Mahatma Gandhi: "What we are doing to the forests of the world is but a mirror reflection of what we are doing to ourselves and to one another." Today, I'm going to talk about how we're treating the rainforests.

1. _____

_____

_____

_____

2. _____

_____

_____

_____

3. _____

_____

_____

_____

Presentation Analysis

Refer to the presentation you chose from Part 1 or choose another presentation. Write the beginning of the presentation here or copy it from the script (if available). Share it and answer these questions.

Opening:

_____

_____

_____

What method(s) did the presenter use? _____

Do you think this was a good choice for the audience and purpose? Why or why not? _____

_____

Rewrite a new opening for the talk using a different strategy.

Your rewrite:

_____

_____

_____

Start Personalizing

Think again about the presentations you listed in the Start Personalizing Box on page 14. Choose one to focus on. What is it?

_____

_____

_____

Which strategy do you think will be the most effective for your intended audience and purpose?

_____

_____

Who is the audience? _____

What is your purpose? _____

Write two potential openings for that presentation.

1. _____

_____

_____

_____

_____

_____

2. _____

_____

_____

_____

_____

_____

Move 2: Flowing through the Presentation (the Body)

After starting the presentation, you begin the body of your speech. Move 2 contains most of your content. Because of this, it is important that you connect the content carefully so that listeners will easily follow the organization and understand the subject matter.

As you progress through your presentation, there are many ways to do this, and the connectors you choose will depend on the way you've chosen to organize the content.

Organizing the Content

There are several ways you can organize the body of your presentation:

- General to specific
- Specific to general
- Descriptive (spatial or compare/contrast)
- Relation (closest to farthest or vice versa)
- Chronological (oldest to newest or vice versa)
- Problem solution (problem description, cause of the problem, recommended solution)
- SPSE (situation, problem, solution, evaluation of two or more solutions)
- Logical (by section; for example, a research presentation could be organized by introduction, methods, results, discussion, conclusion)

You need to choose an organization that will make sense to your listener and for your content. Additionally, you will want to use connecting words and phrases to help your listeners progress from one thought to the next.

Example:

Chronological Order: historical topics, demonstrations, processes or methods, biographical statements (introductions).

■ *Chronological Order Connectors*
after, at that time, before, currently, during, finally, following, meanwhile, next, now, presently, since then, subsequently, then, thereafter, when

There are many ways to organize the body or parts of the body of your presentation. You are likely familiar with some of these if you have taken writing classes. Look at these other lists and some of the common connectors associated with each organizational pattern.

■ *Compare/Contrast Connectors*
alternatively, as with, at the same time, but, comparable to, comparatively, conversely, equally, even so, even though, however, in the same way, instead, just as, likewise, nevertheless, nonetheless, notwithstanding, on the contrary, on the other hand, otherwise, rather, similarly, though, unlike

■ *Cause and Effect Connectors*
accordingly, as a result, because, brings about, cause, consequently, contributes to,

effect, for this reason, hence, if . . . then, in order to, is due to, leads to, reason, result, result in, since, so, so that, stems from, thereby, therefore, thus
■ *Problem and Solution Connectors*
as a result, because, cause, caused by, consequently, for that reason, however, in order to, nevertheless, one way to solve, resulting from, the problem is, since, so that, therefore

TASK 4

Read these excerpts from a speech given by President Barack Obama. Highlight any connectors and indicate the organizational pattern. Note: Add any new ones you find to the lists on pages 32-33.

Excerpts are from his Inaugural Address given on January 20, 2009, from http://obamaspeeches.com.

Forty-four Americans have now taken the presidential oath. The words have been spoken during rising tides of prosperity and the still waters of peace. Yet, every so often the oath is taken amidst gathering clouds and raging storms. At these moments, America has carried on not simply because of the skill or vision of those in high office, but because We the People have remained faithful to the ideals of our forbearers, and true to our founding documents.

Today I say to you that the challenges we face are real. They are serious and they are many. They will not be met easily or in a short span of time. But know this, America—they will be met.

On this day, we gather because we have chosen hope over fear, unity of purpose over conflict and discord.

Our journey has never been one of short-cuts or settling for less. It has not been the path for the faint-hearted—for those who prefer leisure over work, or seek only the pleasures of riches and fame. Rather, it has been the risk-takers, the doers, the makers of things—some celebrated but more often men and women obscure in their labor, who have carried us up the long, rugged path towards prosperity and freedom.

But our time of standing pat, of protecting narrow interests and putting off unpleasant decisions—that time has surely passed. Starting today, we must pick ourselves up, dust ourselves off, and begin again the work of remaking America.

They understood that our power alone cannot protect us, nor does it entitle us to do as we please. Instead, they knew that our power grows through its prudent use; our security emanates from the justness of our cause, the force of our example, the tempering qualities of humility and restraint.

Establishing Flow

Throughout a presentation, you may have to shift topics or add more information, especially in longer presentations where you cover more than one topic or have a lot of details. Imagine graduate students presenting their research: They must shift from introductions to literature reviews to methods and on to results and conclusions, and they must include a large amount of detail in each section. Even though the topic may change, the content all falls into Move 2. Help your listeners keep up by signaling your actions.

- Changing the Topic or Shifting the Focus
  - By the way . . .
  - Keep that in mind as I now talk about . . .
  - Let's shift to . . .
  - Moving on . . .
  - Now let me tell you about . . .
  - Now then . . .
  - Remember that for when . . .
  - So . . .
  - Speaking of . . .
  - Then next . . .
  - You may also be curious about . . .
- Adding Information
  - also
  - and
  - another thing
  - besides that
  - furthermore
  - in addition/additionally

- not only . . . but also
- one more thing
- other(s)
- plus

TASK 5

Look at these excerpts you might hear in science presentations. Identify where the speaker changes topic. Insert a signal phrase to make the transition easier for the listeners. Then add more information about one of the topics. Conduct an internet search to help.

1. You might believe that the electric car is a new invention, but you would be wrong. The first electric cars were actually produced in the 1880s. They were actually quite popular in the early twentieth century. What happened? Cheaper gasoline. In turn, electric cars lost market share to gasoline-powered vehicles. This remained true until more recently. Several countries have offered incentives for their citizens to buy electric cars. Those incentives include tax credits, subsidies, and other monetary rewards . . .

2. Ocean waters cover approximately 70 percent of the Earth's surface. One connected body of salt water is called the World Ocean. Some people say the World Ocean is divided into five smaller oceans. The Pacific Ocean is considered the largest. The Pacific Ocean separates Asia and Australia from North and South America. It covers approximately one-third of the surface of the planet and is much larger than all the land on Earth. It's over

63 million square miles. Try to visualize how large that is. The Atlantic Ocean is the second largest, covering just over 41 million square miles, 20 percent of the Earth's surface, and 29 percent of all the water surface of Earth . . .

Good presentations often include examples and definitions. Of course, these can be visual (we'll talk more about visual aids in Move 3), but they do not need to be. Examples and definitions can be verbal. Presenters should alert listeners to examples and definitions with the proper signal phrasing.

■ Giving Examples
- [as indicated by] the following . . .
- a [good] example is . . .
- for example
- for instance
- including
- specifically/to be specific
- such as
- to illustrate/illustrated by

TASK 6

Help these speakers by adding an example. Conduct a quick internet search to help if you want.

1. There are many fields worth studying within the field of engineering, such as

_____

2. Biology is a natural science that studies many things about living organisms, including

_____

3. Einstein was famous for several theories and concepts. For example,

_____

4. Renaissance art is filled with symbolism. To illustrate, look at

_____

■ Giving Definitions
  o Formal Definitions

Term + Class or Category + Description/Function/ Purpose
- Oxygen is a chemical element that readily forms oxides with many other elements and compounds.

  o Extended Definitions

Term + Class or Category + Description/Function/ Purpose + One or more of these:
- Lists of features or characteristics
- Examples
- Physical description
- Process
- Comparison or contrast to something else

Start Personalizing

Choose one term from your field of study or a field you are interested in and define it.

_____

_____

Some presentations are more interactive, meaning that presenters may stop occasionally and invite the audience members to ask questions or make comments. Think about a professor's lecture in a class. Sometimes professors stop to ask for questions before the lecture is over. More formal presentations may not do this, but it is good to be familiar with the phrases that speakers may use should you wish to check for understanding throughout your presentation.

- Checking for Comprehension
  - Does everyone understand?/Everyone understand?
  - So, did everyone understand that?
  - Is that clear?
  - Does that make sense?/Make sense?
  - Did everyone follow that?/Everyone following?
  - Is everyone with me?/You with me?/ With me?
  - Do you see what I mean?/See what I mean?
  - Does everyone see what I'm saying?/See what I'm saying?

Some are even less formal:

- Okay?
- You know?
- Right?

You could also elicit questions during this move if you choose. Just make sure to keep the content on track and on time.

- Any questions so far?
- Do you have any questions at this time/point?
- You can ask questions anytime.
- Any questions before I move on to the next section?
- Any questions on that point?

TASK 7

Take the definition you wrote in the Start Personalizing box on page 38. Add a comprehension-check phrase to it. Then read it to a partner in class or a friend. Ask them to respond. If they didn't understand the definition, consider rewriting it.

One last thing to remember about the content of your presentation: You need to emphasize the information you believe is most important and convey this to the listeners. While there are some ways to do this using your voice (see the section on pronunciation, page 85), you can also emphasize information by using certain signal words and phrases.

- Emphasizing Information
  - as [unusual] as this sounds
  - as a matter of fact
  - believe it or not

- interestingly
- [oddly] enough
- surprisingly
- the [fascinating] thing is
- this sounds [strange] but
- what I found most [interesting]

TASK 8

Read the following information about storm surges from the National Oceanic and Atmospheric Administration. Imagine someone converting this information into a presentation. Insert at least three emphasizing words and phrases by information you think is the most important.

Introduction

Along the coast, storm surge is often the greatest threat to life and property from a hurricane. In the past, large death tolls have resulted from the rise of the ocean associated with many of the major hurricanes that have made landfall. Hurricane Katrina (2005) is a prime example of the damage and devastation that can be caused by surge. At least 1500 persons lost their lives during Katrina and many of those deaths occurred directly, or indirectly, as a result of storm surge.

Storm Surge vs. Storm Tide

Storm surge is an abnormal rise of water generated by a storm, over and above the predicted astronomical tides. Storm surge should not be confused with storm tide, which is defined as the water level rise due to the combination of storm surge and the astronomical tide. This rise in water level can cause extreme flooding in coastal areas particularly when storm surge coincides with normal high tide, resulting in storm tides reaching up to 20 feet or more in some cases.

Factors Impacting Surge

Storm surge is produced by water being pushed toward the shore by the force of the winds moving cyclonically around the storm. The impact on surge of the low pressure associated with intense storms is minimal in comparison to the water being forced toward the shore by the wind.

The maximum potential storm surge for a particular location depends on a number of different factors. Storm surge is a very complex phenomenon because it is sensitive to the slightest changes in storm intensity, forward speed, size (radius of maximum winds-RMW), angle of approach to the coast, central pressure (minimal contribution in comparison to the wind), and the shape and characteristics of coastal features such as bays and estuaries.

Other factors which can impact storm surge are the width and slope of the continental shelf. A shallow slope will potentially produce a greater storm surge than a steep shelf. For example, a Category 4 storm hitting the Louisiana coastline, which has a very wide and shallow continental shelf, may produce a 20-foot storm surge, while the same hurricane in a place like Miami Beach, Florida, where the continental shelf drops off very quickly, might see an 8 or 9-foot surge. . . .

Adding to the destructive power of surge, battering waves may increase damage to buildings directly along the coast. Water weighs approximately 1,700 pounds per cubic yard; extended pounding by frequent waves can demolish any structure not specifically designed to withstand such forces. The two elements work together to increase the impact on land because the surge makes it possible for waves to extend inland.

Additionally, currents created by tides combine with the waves to severely erode beaches and coastal highways. Buildings that survive hurricane winds can be damaged if their foundations are undermined and weakened by erosion.

In confined harbors, the combination of storm tides, waves, and currents can also severely damage marinas and boats. In estuaries and bayous, salt water intrusion endangers the public health, kills vegetation, and can send animals, such as snakes and alligators, fleeing from flooded areas.

From: https://www.nhc.noaa.gov/surge/

Presentation Analysis

Refer to the presentation you chose from Part 1 or choose another presentation. Print the script. If the presentation you chose does not have a script, choose another from a website that has scripts available, such as TED Talks, NPR, SpeakingFrog, or American Rhetoric Online Speech Bank. Complete these tasks.

1. Who is the intended audience? _____

2. What was the presenter's purpose? _____

3. How is the speech or different parts organized?

_____

4. What type of opening was used? _____

5. Highlight the signal words and phrases the presenter included throughout the presentation and mark what they indicate. Do you think there should be more or less? How does this affect the comprehensibility of the content?

_____

6. Are there any other words or phrases that you think signal something to the listeners? What are they? Add them to the lists in this book. _____

7. What examples (if any) are used? _____

8. What information was emphasized? Do you agree that this information was worth emphasizing? Is there anything else you would emphasize? Mark those by adding emphasis signals.

_____

9. Did you like the presentation? Why or why not?

_____

_____

10. Using your answers to these questions, prepare a short presentation recommending or not recommending this presentation to others.

Start Personalizing

Think again about the presentations you listed in the Start Personalizing box on page 14. Choose one to focus on. What is it?

_____

_____

How to you think you will organize the presentation?

_____

What signal words and phrases do you think will be most useful to you?

_____

Can you write any sentences about your topic that you want to use?

_____

_____

_____

_____

_____

_____

Move 3: Using Visual Aids

Move 3 falls in the middle of the spectrum. Some presenters may begin using visual aids in Move 1 or even before the presentation starts if they display a title slide. Move 3 can continue through Moves 2 and 4 as well. Some presenters might even refer back to their visuals during Move 5 (Q & A). For example, if an audience member asks a question that could benefit from reshowing a slide, the presenter may again display that slide. This section provides language you can use when you are presenting your visual aids and data, which are often best visualized on a slide.

Talking about Data

Many academic presentations are enhanced by and/or require you to cite or support your content with data. In formal talks, you may actually be able to show figures, tables, and charts in slides. For a good discussion on data commentary in writing, read *Academic Writing for Graduate Students* by John M. Swales and Christine B. Feak. Some of this language can be useful in presentations as well. However, even if showing data isn't always possible, you can still talk about results.

Review the phrasing below. Notice how you need to let listeners know whether opinions or ideas are held by the majority or minority, or if they are divided.

- A minority of interviewees . . .
- Most respondents . . .

- Only a small number . . .
- Results were divided among options.
- The majority of . . .
- There was not a clear majority.

Tips for Good Data Presentations

- Make generalizations when need be.
  - From these results, we can generalize that . . .
- Let listeners know when you are surprised.
  - I was surprised to find out that . . .
- Reveal contradictions when they occur.
  - Although I expected the survey to reveal [THIS], I actually learned . . .
- Draw conclusions.
  - The fact that [THIS] proves that . . .
- Indicate movement.
  - There was a rise/increase/improvement/ jump.
  - There was a fall/decrease/decline/drop.
- Indicate stability.
  - Research shows this trend is remaining constant/is stable/leveled off/ plateaued.
- Indicate things are still changing.
  - I don't think we can focus on this result because things are still fluctuating/ changing/moving.
- Indicate the lowest levels.
  - We can't make that our business idea. The sales bottomed out/struck a low.

▪ Indicate the highest level.
- We can't make that our business idea. The sales already peaked/reached their highest point.

Introducing Statistics or Main Ideas about Data

- A recent study shows . . .
- General results indicate . . .
- In the 2020 census, results show that . . .
- Many respondents said that . . .
- Method 1 was right in that [XXX], but it was wrong in that [XXX].
- Other engineers noted that . . .
- Results dictate that . . .
- [Sociologists] tend to believe that . . .
- This new research shows . . .

Referring to Charts, Graphs, or Illustrations

- As shown in the . . .
- As you can see . . .
- Here in this [chart], you can see that . . .
- Let's take a look at this figure . . .
- So you can see that . . .

Referring to Charts, Graphs, or Illustrations That Belong to Others

Sometimes you may want to support your own findings with information from others. Make sure to let your listeners know when you are paraphrasing or summarizing someone else's content. Why would you want to cite others in your presentation?

- Adds credibility to your content
- Adds support
- Persuades your listeners
- Shows your research is grounded in previous research
- Adds examples of other points of view
- Calls attention to or highlights important information
- You can use some of this framing to let your audience members know when you are summarizing someone else.
  - [Smith] acknowledges/agrees/argues/ believes/claims/demonstrates/observes/ supports/reports/suggests that [my method is sound].
  - [Smith] states . . .
  - In [JOURNAL], [Smith] . . .
  - According to [Smith] . . .

Summarizing Your Data

Summarizing is a big part of Move 4, and you will read more about it later. But remember that you may summarize in Moves 2 and 3 as well. You can summarize smaller sections of a presentation before moving on to other sections. Or you can summarize your data and results using visual aids.

- Basically, I'm saying . . .
- By saying this, I'm arguing that . . .
- In other words, my results show . . .

Qualifying Your Claims

It is important that you convey how strongly you are committed to your ideas. When we do this, we are boosting, or letting our listeners know we are confident. When we are less certain, we use hedging to convey to our listeners that we are not as sure. There are several strategies you can use to qualify your claims.

Hedging and Boosting Strategies

- Adjectives
  - almost all, few, little, most, some
- Adverbs
  - likely, often, rarely, somewhat
- Conditionals
  - if/then, under these circumstances, unless, when
- Distancing (attributing claims to others)
  - according to a study; based on limited data; in the view of many experts
- Fractions or percentages
  - half of [our samples], only a few, a small number of
- Modals
  - could, may, might, should
- Prepositional phrases
  - in the long term, in this area, under certain temperatures
- Time expressions
  - currently, now, thus far

- Verb strength
  - appear, cause, seem, show, suggest, indicate

Using Descriptive Words and Phrases

When describing visuals, it is helpful to use descriptive words to help the audience members quickly see what you are referring to.

- Point out colors or size
  - The red line is how much sales decreased.
  - The blue section shows how large the population in China is.
  - The largest/longest bar in this graph shows . . .
- Use spatial words and phrases: above, across (from), adjacent (to), around, after, at, behind, below, beside, between, by, centered, close (to), far (from), in, inside, near, next to, on, outside, over, to the left (of), to the right (of), under
  - The lever closest to machine's start button, which, as you can see here, is centered on the processor, can be used.
  - The two outputs are adjacent to each other on the far right side of the screen.
- Point with your words
  - This is the machine we used to test the samples.
  - Here you have the bacteria that developed when we left the samples overnight.

- These are the spots that form on the surface, and those are the lines that form on the interior.

Suggestions for Using Visual Aids

- Create handouts (not necessarily for all the slides, but a nice summary).
- Check equipment in advance.
- Check the lighting.
- Keep eye contact with the audience, not your visual aid.
- Use a laser, a pointer, your hand, or other cues to make sure the audience members focus on what you want them to see.
- If you write on the board, try to write as much as possible in advance.

Some Tips for Creating Visual Aids

- Keep them simple.
- Make sure images and text are large and clear.
- Add color when possible.
  - Consider colors carefully
    - Examples: Some colors can't be seen as easily by all people, other colors are often difficult to distinguish between on slides (such as blue/purple).

- Remove any wording or text that you do not need, including anything that you will not be including in your presentation.
- Add a title for every slide.
- Label parts (or be prepared to describe them verbally and non-verbally).
- Include any sources or citation information.

TASK 9

Look at this illustration projecting the temperature in August for the United States. Write a few sentences about the image using some of the Move 3 language framing.

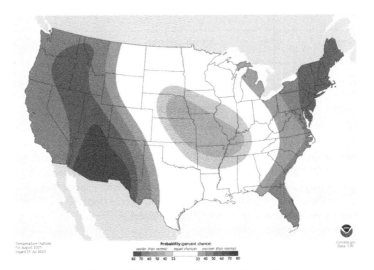

From https://www.climate.gov/maps-data/data-snapshots/tempoutlook-monthly-cpc-2020-07-31?theme=Temperature

---

TASK 10

Look at this data. Create a graph to present the data. Then write a few sentences to describe your chart or graph.

2019–2020 Grant and Loan Volume by School Type*		
	Disbursements	Percentage
Public	$ 54,965,459,003	55.7%
Proprietary	$ 9,416,798,668	9.5%
Private	$ 33,119,690,397	33.6%
Foreign	$ 1,115,991,797	1.1%
Total	$ **98,617,939,865**	

*Data Not Final. Data represents a partial award year as it was calculated using the 2019–2020 FSA Data Center loan and grant files (run April 2020). These files will be updated each quarter to account for additional disbursements and adjustments. This also excludes Campus-Based Programs (Federal Supplemental Educational Opportunity Grants, Perkins Loans, and Federal Work-Study).

From https://studentaid.gov/data-center/student/title-iv

TASK 11

Go to https://geodesy.noaa.gov/web/science_edu/presentations_archive/. Choose a presentation and download the slides. Analyze the slides using this list of suggestions.

Your analysis/opinion of the slides:

_____

_____

_____

Presentation Analysis

Refer to the presentations you have analyzed. Create a slide to go with one presentation. If a slide already exists, then please choose a speech from American Rhetoric (see Appendix) and create a slide using the transcript.

Start Personalizing

Think again about the presentation you have been personalizing. Create one graph, chart, or illustration for your presentation. Write some sentences you can include describing the visual aid. If time allows, create another slide to practice with.

Move 4: Concluding the Presentation (the Conclusion)

The end of a presentation usually includes a summary, but be aware that you might be able to use some of this language throughout your presentation. For example, if you are giving a research presentation, you may include a summary of your methods section. You may also think about describing a chart, graph, or illustration as a summary of sorts.

The language framing listed here can also be used during Move 5, the last things you say before you open the floor for the Q & A. Summarizing your presentation should include your main ideas and key details only. Remember that a summary, like in writing, is significantly shorter than the whole piece. It gives a broad overview of the presentation. What do you want the audience to remember? Most conclusions do *not* need to be very long.

Strategies for Conclusions

- Tie your conclusion to a question you asked or a strategy you used in Move 1.
- Stress the importance of your topic by relating it to the audience members.
- End with a question for people to think about.
- End with a recommendation or call to action.
- Explain what you intend to do in future research.
- Emphasize the importance of your topic/ research.
- Emphasize your main points if necessary.

As you are concluding your speech, it is also common practice to indicate the time and thank the audience members.

First, you may have to signal everyone that the time for your presentation has ended.

Indicating the End

- I know I could keep talking, but my allotted time is nearly over and I want to leave time for questions . . .
- I need to close/stop for today.
- I'm about out of time . . .
- I'm almost out of time . . .
- It's time for me to wrap up.
- This session ends at 5:30 and it's already 5:20. Let me summarize now so that I leave us some time for questions.
- Time is almost up . . .

Then you should summarize the presentation.

Summarizing the Content

- All in all . . .
- In brief . . .
- In conclusion/To conclude . . .
- In short . . .
- In summary/To sum up . . .
- On the whole . . .
- Ultimately . . .

Thanking the Audience Members

It is always nice to thank everyone for their participation.

- I really enjoy [this topic] and I hope you enjoyed hearing about it.
- I'm glad I had the chance to share this.
- I'm happy to take some questions now.
- Thank you.
- Thanks for letting me speak today.
- Thanks for listening.
- Thanks for your attention.

TASK 12

Imagine you had to introduce a well-known person at a conference. Find a biography for any person you are interested in. Write a short summary that you could use as an introduction.

_____

_____

_____

_____

_____

_____

_____

TASK 13

The Three Minute Thesis (3MT®) competition started at The University of Queensland and is now held at many universities around the world. In it, PhD candidates must take years' worth of research and pages from their thesis or dissertation and condense it into a three-minute talk or summary suitable for a non-specialist audience, and they are allowed only one slide. Students are judged on comprehension and content as well as engagement and communication.

Choose a Three Minute Thesis (3MT®) from the Three Minute Thesis (3MT®) site, the Vimeo site, or any you find from an internet search for Three Minute Thesis (3MT®) (choose one from a university you are familiar with or are interested in).

Three Minute Thesis (3MT®) site: https://threeminute thesis.uq.edu.au/watch-3mt

Vimeo site: https://vimeo.com/threeminutethesis

Imagine you are a judge. Judge the performance using the criteria from https://threeminutethesis.uq.edu.au/resources/judging-criteria.

Comprehension and content

- Did the presentation provide an understanding of the background and significance to the research question being addressed, while explaining terminology and avoiding jargon?

- Did the presentation clearly describe the impact and/or results of the research, including conclusions and outcomes?
- Did the presentation follow a clear and logical sequence?
- Was the thesis topic, research significance, results/impact and outcomes communicated in language appropriate to a non-specialist audience?
- Did the presenter spend adequate time on each element of their presentation—or did they elaborate for too long on one aspect or was the presentation rushed?

Engagement and communication

- Did the oration make the audience want to know more?
- Was the presenter careful not to trivialise or generalise their research?
- Did the presenter convey enthusiasm for their research?
- Did the presenter capture and maintain their audience's attention?
- Did the speaker have sufficient stage presence, eye contact and vocal range; maintain a steady pace, and have a confident stance?
- Did the PowerPoint slide enhance the presentation—was it clear, legible, and concise?

TASK 14

Think about your own presentations or presentation goals. Answer these questions.

1. Using the Three Minute Thesis (3MT®) criteria, what questions do you think a judge would answer yes to for you?

   _____

   _____

2. Which performance areas do you think you are strongest at? Why?

   _____

   _____

3. Which do you think you are weakest at? What can you do to improve those?

   _____

   _____

Presentation Analysis

Refer to the presentation you chose from Part 1 or
choose another presentation. Copy the summary of
the presentation from the script or website here (if
available). Share it and answer these questions.

Summary:

_____

_____

_____

_____

What words did the presenter use to capture the
presentation's main ideas?

_____

Do you think this topic was a good choice for the
audience and purpose? Why or why not?

_____

_____

Write a new summary for the talk or choose another talk
and write a summary for it.

Your rewrite:

_____

_____

_____

_____

Start Personalizing

Think again about the presentations you listed in the Start Personalizing box on page 14. List the main points of one presentation that you would need to include in the summary.

_____

_____

Write two potential summaries for that presentation.

_____

_____

_____

_____

_____

Move 5: Managing the Q & A

The Q & A is usually one of the most dreaded parts of a presentation because you simply do not know what people might ask you.

After opening the session with a simple statement like

- Any questions?
- I'm happy to take questions now.
- What questions can I answer?

- I would be happy to entertain questions now.
- If you have a question, please raise your hand.

You need to be prepared to answer (or not answer!) the questions.

Q & A Language

- ◾ Make sure to keep the Q & A moving.
  - Any other questions?
  - Next question?
- ◾ Make sure people know when you are taking the last question.
  - Any last questions?
  - Final questions?
  - I have time for one more question.

It's easy when you know the answer. But what do you do if you don't know the answer?

What to Say When You Don't Know the Answer

Don't be afraid to say you don't know an answer.

- ◾ Compliment the question and then be honest.
  - That's a good question, but I'm actually not sure of the answer.
- ◾ Let them know the scope of your research.
  - Hmmm. I'm not sure my research can answer that.

- Unfortunately, that's beyond the scope of this research
- Offer to find the answer and contact them later.
  - I would have to look that up. Maybe we can exchange contact information and touch base later.
  - I don't know that information off the top of my head, but I can find some good references and send them to you.

What to Say When You Don't Understand or Can't Hear the Question

Don't be afraid to ask for clarification.

- Are you asking me . . . ?
- Can you say that a little slower?
- I'm not sure I understand what you mean by . . .
- I'm sorry, I didn't hear you. Can you say that again?
- I'm sorry, I'm not sure I understand the question. Can you repeat it?

Tips for Q & A

- Leave your last slide with contact information on the screen so people can follow up with you later.

- Ask for questions in advance of the presentation and try to prepare answers for those questions.
- Recognize people by name (when possible) or location/description (when you don't have names and especially when you have a large audience and many hands are raised).
  - Lee has a question. Lee?
  - I see a lot of hands. I think the woman in the blue dress had her hand up first.
  - What about the man in the front row?
- Set up an order when there are many hands raised.
  - Let me start with the man in the front row. Then I'll go to the woman in the back of the room.
- Pause to think about the question and your answer. Hesitations are okay!
- Check for comprehension and repeat questions (restate and reword the questions).
  - Did everyone hear that?
  - The question is . . .
- Answer and move on (keep answers short and simple).
- Stay on topic (answer only the question that was asked).
  - I appreciate the question, but my presentation today focused only on . . .
- Make eye contact with the asker, but present the answer to the whole audience.

- Try to organize your answer.
- Don't pretend to know the answer.
- Announce that a Q & A session will be held at the end if you do not wish to be interrupted during the presentation.
  - I will leave time for questions at the end.

If you are presenting online:

- Have someone monitor the chat box and then pose those questions to you at the end.
- Try to monitor the chat box yourself throughout the presentation.
- Look at the webcam when answering questions.
- Leave your screen share on during Q &A, showing a slide with your contact information.

TASK 15

Answer these questions.

1. Have you ever participated in a Q & A? What was your role (asking questions or answering questions)? How did it go? Was it a positive experience or negative experience?

_____

_____

2. Do you look forward to or dread the Q & A for your own presentations? Why?

_____

_____

3. What makes Q & A challenging both as a presenter and as an audience member?

_____

_____

4. What tips have you used that worked well for managing Q & A?

_____

_____

TASK 16

Watch this video: https://www.press.umich.edu/elt/compsite/4Point/vls22ed_6.mov. Answer these questions.

1. Did the presenter pause or hesitate? Does this bother you? Why or why not?

_____

_____

2. What strategies did the presenter use to manage the Q & A? Do you think these were good? In general, how do you think he did?

_____

_____

3. What did you think of the audience members? What did you think about their attitudes? What did you think of their questions? Would you want these people in your audience?

_____

_____

4. How sure was the presenter about his answers? Did he seem more confident about different questions?

_____

_____

TASK 17

Look at the script from the video. Highlight language the presenter uses that you like. In another color, highlight language the audience members use that you feel is common.

Presenter: Based on the results from my survey and its positive number from the experiment, I am confident that my plan has the potential to revolutionize the way that people use circuits. Thank you. Are there any questions?

Participant: Yes. I appreciate the plan you've put forward, but it seems kind of complicated. If I were to try to replicate this, how many engineers would I need to bring on board?

Presenter: Well, based on my research, six. I know that might sound [like] a lot, but I believe that the benefits will outweigh the costs associated with the high numbers of engineers, and the savings should come in shortly within a year.

Participant: Great. Thanks. Um, I have another question, if you don't mind. You just mentioned costs, but your presentation suggested that, uh, companies would save time as well. Uh, in your opinion, do companies have the resources today to undertake something like this?

Presenter: I don't know, but I certainly hope so. Uh, my survey, which is given to 100 engin, excuse me, from 100 managers of financial and engineering firms, um, indicate that they are willing to, uh, hire new engineers or invest in new circuit systems. And, you may recall from the slide that 62 percent of them have done that and 84 percent of them are willing to try out new teams or systems. So based on this data, I think it's reasonable to assume that the answer to your question is a yes.

Participant: That may be so, but I wonder if small, it's that simple for small companies. Can they afford it? Maybe that's a question that can't be answered yet.

Presenter: Yes, I understand what you are saying, and you are correct in away. Um, but let me address that a bit. In theory, the size of the company really doesn't matter. The implementations and design are really practical. And the cost savings should be recouped shortly after the implementations.

Participant: I really appreciate that you did all this research, but I have another question about the results. You surveyed all the company's managers. But did you survey any of the company's financial managers? Those are the people that control the purse strings. I'm still concerned about the costs.

Presenter: Honestly, I have to check back to see if any of the respondents are COOs or financial managers instead of CEOs. But one point I can add is that in the survey, we ask if any of the companies are willing to participate in a pilot program, and a small number of them actually agreed to that. I was surprised that there weren't more of them, but . . . um, we'll be talking to [these] companies that volunteered, and I hope to present the results of the pilot program in next year's conference.

Participant: I'll look forward to that.

Presenter: Yeah, I think we are off to a good start, and I am cautiously optimistic of the pilot program.

Participant: What will you do next, in terms of the piloting or other research?

Presenter: I will be conducting more experiments and trying to replicate the results.

Participant: Uh, I would like to hear about those before next year's conference so maybe we can stay in contact.

Presenter: That sounds good. Thank you.

Presentation Analysis

Refer to the presentation you chose from Part 1 or choose another presentation.

_____

_____

If the presentation included a Q & A, rate the speaker on how they managed it.

_____

_____

Imagine you were in the audience. What question would you ask?

_____

_____

Write an answer to your own question.

_____

_____

_____

Start Personalizing

Think again about the presentation you listed in the Start Personalizing box on page 14. What questions can you anticipate someone asking during a Q & A?

_____

_____

_____

_____

Prepare answers for those questions.

_____

_____

_____

_____

3

Other Considerations

Overcoming Nervousness

Although there is no surefire way to eliminate nervousness, there are some tips and strategies presenters can try to minimize or lessen their anxiety.

- Practice, practice, practice.
- Practice in front of a mirror.
- Record yourself and evaluate yourself.
- Take an oral presentation or public speaking course.
- Know your topic.
- Be organized. (Prepare, prepare, prepare.)
- Ask a friendly listener to hear your presentation first and provide some feedback.
- Practice the speech in the room or location where the actual presentation will take place (if possible).

- Set up your practice location to look like the room where the presentation will take place (if possible).
- Determine where you are going to stand so you can make the best use of your visual aids and maintain eye contact.
- Plan your non-verbal communication. (See more about non-verbal communication in the next section.)
- Review notes just before your presentation.
- Try some deep breathing exercises or light activity (such as a short walk) before the presentation.
- Focus on the content and not the audience.
- Don't memorize your talk; just speak to your audience.

TASK 18

Check the items that you are nervous about. Add some of your own. Ask someone for tips on how to overcome these challenges.

I'm nervous

_____ my audience won't understand me (pronunciation, voice).

_____ my audience won't understand me (content, vocabulary).

_____ about making eye contact.

_____ my audience will get bored.

_____ I will talk too slow/fast or too softly/loudly.

_____ my visual aids won't work or won't be appropriate.

_____ I won't know the answers during the Q & A.

_____ the technology I need won't work.

_____ I will forget what I'm supposed to say.

_____ I will stand too still/move too much.

_____ _____

_____ _____

Which of the tips and strategies do you want to try? Why?

_____

_____

_____

Which of your anxieties do you most want to address?
Which strategies will help you overcome your
nervousness?

_____

_____

_____

Non-Verbal Communication

Non-verbal communication is extremely important in
any kind of interaction, whether it be social, academic,
or professional. Presentations are no different. Non-
verbal communication can enhance a presentation if

done well. Presenters can use non-verbal language not only to reinforce their words, but also to replace words. Presenters can also use non-verbal cues to gauge their audience members' reactions. Think of the simple example of an audience member raising their hand to let you know they have a question.

Some non-verbal language can negatively impact the presentation. Consider speakers who move their hands too much, sway back and forth or fidget through the presentation, or never make eye contact. Use non-verbal cues to your advantage; avoid non-verbal cues that detract from your message.

There is other non-verbal communication you may not have thought of, such as the colors, hairstyle, and clothing you choose to wear. These details influence your audience's view of you. It's why people usually recommend you wear business attire to a job interview. Also think about other things, such as nervous laughing or chewing gum, that might prove distracting.

Types of Non-Verbal Communication

Gestures

When you use gestures, you use parts of your body, such as hands, arms, or shoulders, in place of or in conjunction with what you are saying. The key to a good presentation is using enough but not too many gestures, as this can be distracting for the audience members. Although there are many types of gestures, there aren't usually as many as there would be in a social conversation or academic discussion.

During a presentation, remember these gestural tips.

- Face your audience.
- Use open body language (don't cross your arms in front of you; in other words, appear "open to" rather than "closed off from" your audience).
- Keep your arms and hands open, palms up.
- Lean toward your audience if possible.
- Use your arms and hands to add clarity or emphasis, but don't get too frenzied with your movements.
- Don't hold anything other than a pointer or laser to indicate your visual aids. You can hold a few note cards if necessary.
- Keep your arms at waist level.
- Keep your elbows loose (not pressed against your body).
- Avoid distracting movements: pulling on your clothing, putting your hands in your pockets, rubbing your hands on your clothes, playing with your hair, playing with objects in your hands, touching your face.
- Avoid grasping your hands behind your back or in front of you and keeping your arms straight at your sides.
- Use rhythmic motions with your hands for emphasis.

■ Mimic actions you are describing when possible.

■ Indicate size and shape with your hands.

■ Use your hands to point at visuals.

■ Use your fingers to count (start with your index finger).

TASK 19

Think of gestures you've used or noticed during a presentation. Share your gestures with a partner. Have your partner guess what they mean.

Movement and Space

Some presenters move around during their presentation. It isn't required, and some decisions about movement might depend on the setting. But movement can be beneficial. Here are some things to think about.

■ Face your audience.

■ Avoid turning your back to look at your visual aids.

■ Move for a reason (don't move for the sake of moving).

■ Stand straight, tall, and balanced.

■ Appear relaxed and confident.

■ Move slowly when you do move (nothing rushed or jerky).

■ If you are speaking from a lectern or podium, make sure to use gestures above the height of the lectern, or occasionally move to stand beside the lectern or podium.

■ Stand ten to twelve feet from your audience (dependent on location, audience size, and level of intimacy you want to convey).

TASK 20

Think of movements you've used or noticed during a presentation. Share what you've liked and disliked about movement.

Eye Contact

Eye contact in some cultures, such as U.S. culture, is very important, so always consider who is in your audience and where you are presenting. What constitutes eye contact during a presentation? You can't look each person in the eye at the same time while you are presenting. It helps engage your audience if you make occasional eye contact with the members. It can be challenging, especially if you are from a culture in which it is respectful to not look directly at others (for example, in cultures where people do not look into the eyes of those who have higher status).

In a presentation, eye contact is necessary to be successful. Here are some dos and don'ts.

■ Do look at the audience. Do not look at the floor or ceiling. Do not look out the window or door.

■ Do glance at your notes or visual aids. Do not read them word for word.

■ Do establish eye contact with various people or various sections around the room. Do not focus on just one person. If you are online, look at the webcam!

- Do hold eye contact for about three to five seconds before moving to the next person. Do not look too long or too fleetingly at one person.
- Do make eye contact deliberate. Do not dart your eyes from person to person too quickly.

Strategies for Eye Contact Practice

- Practice with strangers.
- Practice while being a listener or audience member.
- Have a staring contest with a friend or family member.
- Observe how other presenters and speakers make eye contact.
- Slowly increase the amount of eye contact you make.
- Look around the eyes rather than directly into the eyes (top of someone's nose, bottom of their forehead).
- Practice, practice, practice.

TASK 21

Set a timer for thirty seconds. Work with a partner. Stare at each other until the timer goes off. Remember that if you can last thirty seconds, then five seconds will seem easy. Switch partners and practice this several times.

Facial Expressions

Facial expressions are another key element to a successful presentation. Again, you might not use as many

as you would in a social conversation, but here is what
helps when giving a presentation:

- Smile.
- Change your facial expression (try not to
  maintain a serious or unchanging expression).
- Relax the muscles in your face. Avoid
  looking tense.
- Nod for emphasis.
- Make sure your facial expressions match the
  content.
- When speaking online, facial expressions are
  even more important because you can't use
  gestures or movement.
- Be authentic.
- Avoid touching your face.
- Make sure everyone can see you. If you are in
  a large room, you might need to exaggerate
  your facial expressions or add gestures or
  tone of voice cues to help.
- Use the some of the facial expressions for
  universal emotions that are not usually
  dependent on culture or language when and
  if they are appropriate: happiness, sadness,
  surprise, contempt or dislike, and anger.

The following table lists these as well as some other facial
expressions you might find useful. Remember, you also
want to notice these in your audience as well; this can
help guide you as you present or manage the Q & A.

Universal Emotion	Facial Expression
Happiness	Smiling (mouth corners raised)
Sadness	Frowning (mouth corners lowered)
Surprise	Rounded mouth (mouth open, jaw dropped) Eyebrows raised Eyes widened Tipped head
Contempt or Dislike	Rolling eyes Looking "down your nose" Wrinkled nose
Anger	Closed mouth (lips in straight line) Eyebrows lowered Sneering Pouting Squinting
Other Emotions	**Facial Expression**
Frustration	Upper lip raised Wrinkled forehead or nose Clenched teeth
Support or Agreement	Smiling (accompanied by nodding)
Disagreement	Frowning (accompanied by shaking head) Lips pulled up on one side Eyes partly closed Smirking One eyebrow raised Sideways glance Grimacing Wincing
Concern or Confusion	Pursed lips
Interest	Slightly tipped head Hand on chin

TASK 22

Practice each of the facial expressions in the table. Then write a few notes about which ones are easiest to understand, which ones are more challenging to understand, which ones you think are most important, and which ones you most want to be able to show (as an audience member) and recognize (as a speaker).

_____

_____

_____

_____

_____

_____

TASK 23

Answer these questions.

1. Do you use non-verbal communication when you communicate? When you present? What about when you are a listener or in the audience?

   _____

   _____

2. What types of non-verbal communication
do you do well? What types do you want to
improve?

_____

_____

3. In which circumstances might non-verbal
communication be different? In other words,
what factors might affect the type or amount
of non-verbal communication that is used?
(Example: size of the room.)

_____

_____

Pronunciation and Paralinguistics

Pronunciation is an essential part of participating in
any type of interaction, so it's important in presentations, too. What good is a presentation if no one can
understand you? Paralinguistics are features of verbal
language that do not involve words, but they add meaning or emphasis, such as stress, pitch, tone, pace, or volume. Here are some pronunciation and paralinguistic
notes you should be familiar with and consider when
you are presenting.

Hesitations

What do you do when you just don't know what to say? This might come into play most prevalently in Move 5, the Q & A, because you do not always know what someone is going to ask. Sometimes, though, you just need a moment to collect your thoughts or frame what you want to say next. When someone asks you a question after a presentation, you can't ignore the question. You have no choice but to answer, and you want to think of your answer before you start speaking. Most audience members don't mind if you need a few moments before you begin. You can't wait for a long time, but a short hesitation is okay. Non-verbal cues can help. For example, if you nod your head, tip your head, or touch your chin, all common signs that someone is thinking, this shows the audience that you are formulating your answer. These non-verbal cues can be of less help in online communication since not everything can be seen on a tiny screen or through bad reception. Therefore, giving some sort of verbal cue in conjunction with non-verbal cues is beneficial. The verbal cue doesn't have to be much; the key is that it is verbal and the listeners can hear it.

Some verbal cues you might hear are:

- Alright . . .
- Basically . . .
- Give me a second.
- Good question.
- Hmmm.

- Let me think . . .
- Let's see . . .
- . . . like . . .
- That's a good question.
- Uhhh . . .
- Umm . . .
- Well . . .
- Well, it's hard to know where to start . . .
- You know . . .
- You see . . .
- [other sounds—clicking or clucking tongue, er, ah]

■ Or some combination:
  - Well, hmmm, give me a second . . .
■ Or use a hesitation before letting the listener know you are attempting an answer or giving your opinion:
  - Well, I'm not sure, but I think . . .
■ Note: Sometimes a hesitation device could be said longer or more slowly:
  - Weeeeellllll . . .

One thing to remember is that hesitation devices are sometimes a sign of lacking knowledge or speaking skills, but *not* always. Sometimes they really are just a marker that you are framing your idea. It's often better to let the person know you heard them and are participating than to not verbalize anything at all. Always remember that saying something is better than worrying about perfect grammar or pronunciation.

TASK 24

Answer these questions with a partner.

1. Which hesitation devices do you think might be better than others? Why do you think so?

_____

_____

2. How many hesitation devices do you use? Could you use more or fewer? Have you noticed native speakers using hesitation devices?

_____

_____

3. How can you achieve a goal of using fewer hesitations?

_____

_____

Pausing

While too much hesitating is not always a good thing, some pausing is natural and acceptable. You need to find the right balance. If you speak too slowly, with too many pauses, you sound unprepared. If you talk too quickly, you sound nervous and may be incomprehensible. You should try to gather your words into thought groups to avoid too many or too few pauses.

Thought Groups

A thought group is a set of words that go together to express an idea. For example, the phrase *at Stanford University* is a prepositional phrase—or thought group—that conveys location.

> ▦ *Lee is teaching engineering at Stanford University. His research field is hardware engineering. Before joining Stanford, Lee worked at a large engineering firm in Silicon Valley.*

With pauses after thought groups:

> ▦ *Lee is teaching engineering [pause] at Stanford University [pause]. His research field [pause] is hardware engineering [pause]. Before joining Stanford [pause], Lee worked at a large engineering firm [pause] in Silicon Valley.*

When to pause:

- ▦ after thought groups
- ▦ at the ends of sentences
- ▦ at topic shifts

TASK 25

Read the end of the commencement address Steve Jobs delivered at Stanford University. Add // at each place you think a pause should be. Then take turns reading it aloud with a partner. Answer the questions when you finish working with your partner.

> Your time is limited, so don't waste it living someone else's life. Don't be trapped by dogma—which is living with the results of other people's thinking. Don't let the noise of others' opinions drown out your own inner voice. And most important, have the courage to follow your heart and intuition. They somehow already know what you truly want to become. Everything else is secondary.

> When I was young, there was an amazing publication called *The Whole Earth Catalog*, which was one of the bibles of my generation. It was created by a fellow named Stewart Brand not far from here in Menlo Park, and he brought it to life with his poetic touch. This was in the late 1960s, before personal computers and desktop publishing, so it was all made with typewriters, scissors, and Polaroid cameras. It was sort of like Google in paperback form, 35 years before Google came along: It was idealistic, and overflowing with neat tools and great notions.

> Stewart and his team put out several issues of *The Whole Earth Catalog*, and then when it had run its course, they put out a final issue. It was the mid-1970s, and I was your age. On the back cover of their final issue was a photograph of an early morning country road, the kind you might find yourself hitchhiking on

if you were so adventurous. Beneath it were the words: "Stay Hungry. Stay Foolish." It was their farewell message as they signed off. Stay Hungry. Stay Foolish. And I have always wished that for myself. And now, as you graduate to begin anew, I wish that for you.

Stay Hungry. Stay Foolish.

Thank you all very much.

1. Did you and your partner mark the same places? What was the same? What was different?

_____

_____

2. Did you hear the pauses when your partner read? Did your partner hear your pauses? What can you do to improve?

_____

_____

3. Find a video of Steve Jobs delivering his speech. Mark the speech again when he pauses. Do his pauses match yours? Do you think he paused too much, too little, or just right? Did he speak too slowly or too quickly?

_____

_____

Volume

Presenters need to make sure they are speaking loudly enough so that everyone can hear them, especially if they do not have a microphone or if they are presenting online. Volume can also enhance clarity or pronunciation.

Stress (Word and Sentence)

Word Stress

Multisyllabic words in English have one syllable that is stressed more than the others. The stress falls over the vowel in a word. You say the syllable louder, longer, and with a different pitch to stress it. There are many rules associated with word stress. For example, the stress in most words that end in –al falls on the third to last syllable.

ex-CEP-tion-al   CRI-ti-cal

All the word stress rules can't be covered in this book. Consult a good pronunciation book and familiarize yourself with some general rules, such as stressing the first syllable of most two-syllable nouns (CLI-mate or PRES-ent) and the second syllable of most two-syllable verbs (de-CIDE or pre-SENT). Review the rules that most apply to you.

TASK 26

Make a list of words common in your field of study or words you struggle to say. Determine which syllable should be stressed.

_____

_____

_____

TASK 27

Look up how to pronounce words with these suffixes in English. Write one or two sample words.

Example:

–ic   stress one syllable before the suffix   classic or specific

    1. –tion or –sion

    2. –ity

    3. –phy

    4. –eer

    5. –ate

    6. –ible

    7. –ate

    8. –ify

    9. –ogy

    10. –ize

Sentence Stress

In English, certain words in a sentence are emphasized more than others. Again, there are some general rules, but emphasis also allows the speaker to express which word they feel is the most important. Emphasize or give prominence to certain syllables in words or to certain words in a sentence. This helps your listeners understand the word or what you feel is the most important word in a statement. The word you stress can dramatically change the meaning of a sentence.

Compare these statements (capital letters indicate stress).

I did not say you could come to the party! (Someone else said that.)

I did **NOT** say that you could come to the party! (I deny saying that.)

I did not **SAY** that you could come to the party! (But maybe I thought it!)

I did not say that **YOU** could come to the party! (But I did say someone else could!)

I did not say that you **COULD** come to the party! (Of course you can come to the party!)

I did not say that you could **COME** to the party! (I said you could help plan the party!)

I did not say that you could come to the **PARTY**! (I said you could come to the dinner!)

Like word stress, to add stress to a sentence, say the stressed word louder, longer, and with a higher pitch.

In general, stress words that contain the most meaning, and do not stress words that are simply performing a function and don't hold as much meaning. (Unless, of course, one of those "small" words wasn't heard and caused a misunderstanding: No, not the book ON the shelf. The one UNDER the shelf.) Function words are more for grammar and not meaning. Again, saying something is better than not talking at all. Don't worry about perfect pronunciation.

Stress CONTENT words	Do not stress FUNCTION words
Nouns	Pronouns
Verbs	Prepositions
Adjectives	Conjunctions
Adverbs	Articles
Question words	Determiners
Negatives	Auxiliary verbs
Numbers or words you need for quality or quantity	Forms of the "be" verb

TASK 28

Write a few examples of each item in the chart.

Stress CONTENT words	Examples	Do not stress FUNCTION words	Examples
Nouns		Pronouns	
Verbs		Prepositions	
Adjectives		Conjunctions	
Adverbs		Articles	

Stress CONTENT words	Examples	Do not stress FUNCTION words	Examples
Question words		Determiners	
Negatives		Auxiliary verbs	
Numbers or words you need for quality or quantity		Forms of the "be" verb	

TASK 29

Read the first part of Martin Luther King Jr.'s "I Have a Dream" speech. Mark which words you want to stress. Then read it to a partner. Have your partner mark which words they hear you stress. Compare your scripts. Then answer the questions.

> I am happy to join with you today in what will go down in history as the greatest demonstration for freedom in the history of our nation.

> Five score years ago, a great American, in whose symbolic shadow we stand today, signed the Emancipation Proclamation. This momentous decree came as a great beacon light of hope to millions of Negro slaves who had been seared in the flames of withering injustice. It came as a joyous daybreak to end the long night of their captivity.

> But one hundred years later, the Negro still is not free. One hundred years later, the life of the Negro is still sadly crippled by the manacles of segregation and the chains of

discrimination. One hundred years later, the Negro lives on a lonely island of poverty in the midst of a vast ocean of material prosperity. One hundred years later, the Negro is still languished in the corners of American society and finds himself an exile in his own land. And so we've come here today to dramatize a shameful condition.

In a sense we've come to our nation's capital to cash a check. When the architects of our republic wrote the magnificent words of the Constitution and the Declaration of Independence, they were signing a promissory note to which every American was to fall heir. This note was a promise that all men, yes, black men as well as white men, would be guaranteed the "unalienable Rights" of "Life, Liberty and the pursuit of Happiness." It is obvious today that America has defaulted on this promissory note, insofar as her citizens of color are concerned. Instead of honoring this sacred obligation, America has given the Negro people a bad check, a check which has come back marked "insufficient funds."

But we refuse to believe that the bank of justice is bankrupt. We refuse to believe that there are insufficient funds in the great vaults of opportunity of this nation. And so, we've come to cash this check, a check that will give us upon demand the riches of freedom and the security of justice.

We have also come to this hallowed spot to remind America of the fierce urgency of Now. This is no time to engage in the luxury of cooling off or to take the tranquilizing drug of gradualism. Now is the time to make real the promises of democracy. Now is the time to rise from the dark and desolate valley of segregation to the sunlit path of racial justice. Now is the time to lift our nation from the quicksands of racial injustice to the solid rock of brotherhood. Now is the time to make justice a reality for all of God's children.

It would be fatal for the nation to overlook the urgency of the moment. This sweltering summer of the Negro's legitimate discontent will not pass until there is an invigorating autumn of freedom and equality. Nineteen sixty-three is not an end, but a beginning. And those who hope that the Negro needed to blow off steam and will now be content will have a rude awakening if the nation returns to business as usual. And there will be neither rest nor tranquility in America until the Negro is granted his citizenship rights. The whirlwinds of revolt will continue to shake the foundations of our nation until the bright day of justice emerges.

1. Did your partner mark the same words you thought you stressed? What was the same? What was different?

2. Why might your partner not have heard what
   you intended to say? What can you do to
   improve your stress patterns?

   _____

   _____

3. Did you correctly identify your partner's
   stresses? Why is it important to be able to hear
   someone's stresses when they are presenting?

   _____

   _____

Pitch

Your voice should rise and fall when you speak.

- If you use a higher pitch, the statement is
  usually positive.
  - My presentation today is about the
    chemical balances in the human brain. (↑)
- If you use a lower pitch, the statement is
  usually negative.
  - Unfortunately, there is still much to be
    learned to help people with chemical
    imbalances. (↓)

Tone

Tone expresses a speaker's attitude and conveys meaning
behind the word choice. Even if you say the "right" words,
if your tone is negative, it could hurt the interaction.

TASK 30

For each of these statements you might say during a discussion, say them using different stresses, pitches, and tones. Which way communicates your intent?

> *My results show just one deficit.*
>
> > *More research needs to be conducted to determine the best way to move forward.*
> >
> > *Solar power is expensive in terms of both money and time.*
> >
> > *In my presentation, I will cover both the pros and cons.*
> >
> > *Although the economy is important, I think we should focus on vaccines.*

Pace

A moderate speed is best in a presentation. You don't want to talk too slowly or too quickly. You can also use pace to convey more meaning. Speaking some words slowly will add emphasis or draw attention. Speaking other words more quickly can convey excitement or passion.

TASK 31

Think of things you have said or heard in a presentation. Practice saying them with the appropriate pronunciation and paralinguistics. Write one example down to read to a partner.

_____

_____

_____

_____

Presentation Analysis

Refer to the presentation you chose from Part 1 or choose another presentation you have analyzed throughout this book. Analyze the speaker's non-verbal and verbal cues. Rank them on a scale of 1 to 5 and give a reason for your score.

Feature	Ranking					Reason
Gestures	1	2	3	4	5	_____
Movement/Space	1	2	3	4	5	_____
Eye Contact	1	2	3	4	5	_____
Facial Expressions	1	2	3	4	5	_____
Hesitations	1	2	3	4	5	_____
Pausing	1	2	3	4	5	_____
Thought Groups	1	2	3	4	5	_____
Volume	1	2	3	4	5	_____
Stress	1	2	3	4	5	_____
Pitch	1	2	3	4	5	_____
Tone	1	2	3	4	5	_____
Pace	1	2	3	4	5	_____

Start Personalizing

Think again about the presentations you listed in the
Start Personalizing box on page 14. Keep developing one
of those presentations. Which one is it?

_____

_____

What non-verbal cues do you want to incorporate?

_____

_____

What verbal or paralinguistics do you want to use?

_____

_____

Write one paragraph of your presentation here. Then
practice reading it with non-verbal and paralinguistics
before reading it to a partner. Ask your partner to
evaluate your non-verbal and verbal language. If you're
not in class, record it and evaluate yourself or submit it
to your instructor for feedback.

_____

_____

_____

_____

_____

_____

4

Presentation Projects

This section of the book includes several types of presentations you can develop to practice the moves, language, and other non-verbal and verbal cues. You can practice these throughout the book. For example, you can give a presentation after each move, focusing on developing just the content in that section. Or, you can complete these projects after reading the book, incorporating all the content into the presentations. If you're studying in class, your teacher might choose some of these or incorporate other types of presentations. All presentations follow the same guidelines.

Introduction Presentation (Self)

Purpose: Introduce yourself.

Time: [X] minutes: _____

Audience: _____ (classmates, colleagues)

Organization/Outline:
Move 1:

Move 2:

Move 3:

Move 4:

Move 5:

Information to include:

Introduction Presentation (Classmate)

Purpose: Introduce a classmate.

Time: [X] minutes: _____

Audience: _____ (classmates, colleagues)

Information to include:

Organization/Outline:

Move 1:

Move 2:

Move 3:

Move 4:

Move 5:

Interview Questions to Ask: Notes:

Introduction Presentation (Guest Speaker/Colleague)

Option: Introduce a famous person.

Purpose: Introduce a guest speaker or colleague.

Time: [X] minutes: _____

Audience: _____ (classmates, colleagues)

Organization/Outline:

Move 1:

Move 2:

Move 3:

Move 4:

Move 5 (not common for an introduction like this):

Information from biography or other online sources (degrees, work history, current work, research interest, publications, awards and honors, etc.):

Panel Presentation

Plan to participate in a panel discussion with a group on [DATE].

In advance of your date, complete this checklist and prepare notes.

_____ Brainstorm topics.

_____ Choose and formulate a topic.

_____ Choose a moderator.

_____ Choose panelists to speak on different aspects of the topic.

_____ Prepare for the general procedure:
* Moderator introduces topic and panelists.
* Moderator provides introduction of topic and panelists.
* Moderator poses question.
* Panelists discuss and make comments on each other's points.
* Moderator controls topic and panelists.
* Moderator briefly summarizes.

_____ Prepare for the Q & A from the audience.

_____ Prepare notes. (Note: Panels are like conversations in front of an audience. They need not have prepared presentations or serious research, but some preparation is helpful to familiarize yourself with the topic, prepare for questions, and plan points you want to make.)

_____ Review phrasing you will need.

_____ Manage the time limits. (Example: 20 to 30 minutes to present information; 15 to 20 minutes for a forum period in which the audience will answer questions or make comments.)

Three Minute Thesis (3MT®) or Elevator Pitch

Prepare a Three Minute Thesis (3MT®) about your research. Follow the same rules as the competition, available at https://threeminutethesis.uq.edu.au/resources/competition-rules.

- A single static PowerPoint slide is permitted. No slide transitions, animations, or "movement" of any description are allowed. The slide is to be presented from the beginning of the oration.
- No additional electronic media (e.g., sound and video files) are permitted.
- No additional props (e.g., costumes, musical instruments, laboratory equipment) are permitted.
- Presentations are limited to three minutes maximum; competitors exceeding three minutes are disqualified.
- Presentations are to be spoken word (e.g., no poems, raps, or songs).
- Presentations are to commence from the stage.
- Presentations are considered to have commenced when a presenter starts their presentation through either movement or speech.

■ Use the suggestions available at https://
threeminutethesis.uq.edu.au/resources/3mt-
competitor-guide as you prepare.

Write for your audience

■ Avoid jargon and academic language.
■ Explain concepts and people important to
your research—you may know all about
Professor Smith's theories, but your audience
may not.
■ Highlight the outcomes of your research, and
the desired outcome.
■ Imagine that you are explaining your
research to a close friend or fellow student
from another field.
■ Convey your excitement and enthusiasm for
your subject.

Tell a story

■ You may like to present your 3MT as a
narrative, with a beginning, middle and end.
■ It's not easy to condense your research into
three minutes, so you may find it easier to
break your presentation down into smaller
sections.
■ Try writing an opener to catch the attention
of the audience, then highlight your different
points, and finally have a summary to restate
the importance of your work.

Have a clear outcome in mind

- Know what you want your audience to take away from your presentation.
- Try to leave the audience with an understanding of what you're doing, why it is important, and what you hope to achieve.

Revise

- Proof your 3MT presentation by reading it aloud, to yourself and to an audience of friends and family.
- Ask for feedback.
- Ask your audience if your presentation clearly highlights what your research is about and why it is important.

Rules

Before you start work on your slide, you should take the following rules into account:

- One single static PowerPoint slide is permitted;
- No slide transitions, animations, or "movement" of any description are permitted;
- Your slide is to be presented from the beginning of your oration; and

- No additional electronic media (e.g., sound and video files) are permitted.

Suggestions

You may like to consider some of the following suggestions.

- **Less is more:** Text and complicated graphics can distract your audience—you don't want them to read your slide instead of listening to your 3MT.
- **Personal touches:** Personal touches can allow your audience to understand the impact of your research.
- **Creativity drives interest:** Do not rely on your slide to convey your message—it should simply complement your oration.
- **Work your message:** Think about how your slide might be able to assist with the format and delivery of your presentation—is there a metaphor that helps explain your research?
- An engaging visual presentation can make or break any oration, so make sure your slide is **legible, clear, and concise**.

Practice, practice, practice

- Feeling nervous before you present is natural, and a little nervousness can even be beneficial to your overall speech. Nonetheless, it is important to practice so you can present with confidence and clarity. Practicing will also help you gauge the timing of your 3MT so that you keep within the time limit.

Vocal range

- Speak clearly and use variety in your voice (fast/slow, loud/soft).
- Do not rush—find your rhythm.
- Remember to pause at key points as it gives the audience time to think about what you are saying.

Body language

- Stand straight and confidently.
- Hold your head up and make eye contact.
- Never turn your back to the audience.
- Practice how you will use your hands and move around the stage. It is okay to move around energetically if that is your personality, however it is also appropriate for a 3MT presentation to be delivered from a single spot on stage.
- Do not make the common mistakes of rolling back and forth on your heels, pacing for no reason, or playing with your hair as these habits are distracting for the audience.

Record yourself

- Record and listen to your presentation to hear where you pause, speak too quickly, or get it just right.
- Then work on your weaknesses and exploit your strengths.

Look to the stars!

- Watch your role models such as academics, politicians, and journalists, and break down their strengths and weaknesses.
- Analyze how they engage with their audience.
- View presentations by previous 3MT finalists.

Dress

- There is no dress code, if you are unsure of how to dress you may like to dress for a job interview or an important meeting. It is important that you feel comfortable so you can focus on your presentation.
- If you are presenting on a stage that has a wooden floor, be aware of the noise your footwear might make.
- Do not wear a costume of any kind as this is against the rules (as is the use of props).

You will be evaluated using the judging criteria from https://threeminutethesis.uq.edu.au/resources/judging-criteria.

Comprehension and content

- Did the presentation provide an understanding of the background and significance to the research question being addressed, while explaining terminology and avoiding jargon?
- Did the presentation clearly describe the impact and/or results of the research, including conclusions and outcomes?
- Did the presentation follow a clear and logical sequence?
- Was the thesis topic, research significance, results/impact and outcomes communicated in language appropriate to a non-specialist audience?
- Did the presenter spend adequate time on each element of their presentation—or did they elaborate for too long on one aspect or was the presentation rushed?

Engagement and communication

- Did the oration make the audience want to know more?
- Was the presenter careful not to trivialise or generalise their research?
- Did the presenter convey enthusiasm for their research?
- Did the presenter capture and maintain their audience's attention?
- Did the speaker have sufficient stage presence, eye contact and vocal range; maintain a steady pace, and have a confident stance?
- Did the PowerPoint slide enhance the presentation—was it clear, legible, and concise?

Definition Presentation

Purpose: Provide an extended definition of a concept from your field of study.

Time: [X] minutes: _____

Audience: _____ (classmates, colleagues)

Considerations:
- Remember your audience may be non-specialists.
- Get the audience engaged.
- Be able to correctly pronounce and stress the term or concept.
- Use visual aids.
- Start with a clear, concise, formal definition of the term or concept.
- Develop or extend using other strategies to make sure your audience members will understand. Organize well.
- Incorporate connectors and other useful language from this book as you plan the moves.
- Anticipate questions.

Data or Results Presentation

Purpose: Describe data and use visual aids.

Time: [X] minutes: _____

Audience: _____ (classmates, colleagues)

Considerations:
- Add titles to visual aids.
- Make sure there is not too much written on the slides.
- Make sure writing and visuals are large enough.
- Label appropriately.
- Make sure the visuals are not too cluttered or confusing.
- Work to make the visual eye-catching.
- Eliminate any content from the visual that you do not present.
- Use appropriate language and framing.
- Organize well.
- Anticipate questions.

Process Presentation

Purpose: Describe a process in your field of study.

Time: [X] minutes: _____

Audience: _____ (classmates, colleagues)

Considerations:

- Remember your audience may be non-specialists.
- Get the audience members engaged. Decide what background information they need.
- Use chronological order and connectors.
- Decide between active and passive voice.
- Use the best modals.
- Use visual aids and non-verbal communication to help explain the steps.
- Incorporate connectors and other useful language from this book as you plan the moves.
- Anticipate questions.

Other Presentation Projects

1. Give an informative speech.
2. Prepare a demonstration or process presentation.
3. Sell a product or service to the rest of the group.
4. Give a persuasive speech.
5. Summarize methods and/or results of your research.
6. Plan a poster or overview of your research for a research group meeting or poster session.
7. Conduct a survey, collect data, and prepare a presentation about the results and your conclusions.
8. Give a problem-solution speech.
9. Describe an object speech. (Option: Describe an object without naming the object, with the goal being to describe it so well that the audience members can guess what it is).
10. Give an impromptu speech.
11. Watch or attend a presentation on campus. Prepare a report or watch a video of it with the class. Evaluate the speaker and the content.
12. Give a compare/contrast speech.
13. Describe a research study famous in your field.

14. Summarize a book or article.
15. Record any of your projects and peer and self-evaluate.
16. Prepare a research presentation for a conference or dissertation defense with these parts: Introduction, Methodology, Results, and Discussion. Include the purpose of your research and a literature review in your introduction.

■ Appendix: Rubrics and Evaluation Forms

General Presentation Evaluation Form (adaptable per presentation)

Name of Presenter:

_____

Audience (who was it for and was that achieved)
5   4   3   2   1
Purpose (what was it for and was that achieved)
5   4   3   2   1
Organization (overall and within sections)
5   4   3   2   1

Move 1
5   4   3   2   1
Move 2
5   4   3   2   1
Move 3
5   4   3   2   1
Move 4
5   4   3   2   1
Move 5
5   4   3   2   1

Non-verbal (gestures, movement and space, eye contact, facial expressions)

5   4   3   2   1

Paralinguistics (hesitations, pausing, thought groups, volume, stress, pitch, tone, pace)

5   4   3   2   1

Other Notes

Self-Evaluation: What do you want to do better?

Peer Evaluation: Your peer evaluator said . . .

Grade

Panel Presentation Moderator

Task	1 to 5 Rating	Comments
Introduction of topic		
Introduction of panelists		
Background information		
Maintained flow		
Used appropriate phrasing		
Managed time		
Summarized		
Volume		
Eye contact		
General pronunciation notes		
General vocabulary notes		
General non-verbal communication notes		
General grammar notes		

Panel Presentation Panelist

Task	1 to 5 Rating	Comments
Contributed equally		
Contributions were relevant and important		
Background information		
Answered when called on		
Jumped in as necessary		
Used appropriate phrasing		
Volume		
Eye contact		
General pronunciation notes		
General vocabulary notes		
General non-verbal communication notes		
General grammar notes		

Three Minute Thesis (3MT®) Judging Criteria from https://threeminutethesis.uq.edu.au/resources/ judging-criteria

Comprehension and content

- Did the presentation provide an understanding of the background and significance to the research question being addressed, while explaining terminology and avoiding jargon?
- Did the presentation clearly describe the impact and/or results of the research, including conclusions and outcomes?
- Did the presentation follow a clear and logical sequence?
- Was the thesis topic, research significance, results/impact and outcomes communicated in language appropriate to a non-specialist audience?
- Did the presenter spend adequate time on each element of their presentation—or did they elaborate for too long on one aspect or was the presentation rushed?

Engagement and communication

- Did the oration make the audience want to know more?
- Was the presenter careful not to trivialise or generalise their research?
- Did the presenter convey enthusiasm for their research?
- Did the presenter capture and maintain their audience's attention?
- Did the speaker have sufficient stage presence, eye contact and vocal range; maintain a steady pace, and have a confident stance?
- Did the PowerPoint slide enhance the presentation—was it clear, legible, and concise?

◼ Extra Reading

Boldt, H. (2019). *The Three Minute Thesis in the Classroom: What Every ESL Teacher Needs to Know.* University of Michigan Press.

Carnegie, D., & Esenwein, J. B. (2007). *The Art of Public Speaking.* Cosimo. (Original work published 1915)

Lockwood, R. B. (2020). *Leading Academic Discussions: What Every University Student Needs to Know.* University of Michigan Press.

Lockwood, R. B. (2019). *Office Hours: What Every University Student Needs to Know.* University of Michigan Press.

Lockwood, R. B. (2018). *Speaking in Social Contexts: Communication for Life and Study in the United States.* University of Michigan Press.

Reinhart, S. (2013). *Giving Academic Presentations.* University of Michigan Press.

Swales, J., & Feak, C. (2012). *Academic Writing for Graduate Students.* University of Michigan Press.

Public Speaking Websites

American Rhetoric: www.americanrhetoric.com

National Speakers Association: www.nsaspeaker.org

Public Speakers Association: https://publicspeakers association.com/

TED Talks: www.ted.com

Toastmasters International: https://www.toastmasters. org/

Printed and bound by CPI Group (UK) Ltd, Croydon, CR0 4YY

13/04/2025

14656531-0003

.